Imagination comes alive in Express! Transform the everyday into the fresh and new, discover ways to stir up flavor and excitement, and experiment with new ideas and materials. Express! makerspace books: where your next creative adventure begins!

This edition first published in 2023 by Bellwether Media, Inc.

No part of this publication may be reproduced in whole or in part without written permission of the publisher. For information regarding permission, write to Bellwether Media, Inc., Attention: Permissions Department, 6012 Blue Circle Drive, Minnetonka, MN 55343.

Library of Congress Cataloging-in-Publication Data

LC record for Throw a Lunar New Year Party available at: https://lccn.loc.gov/2022047988

Text copyright © 2023 by Bellwether Media, Inc. EXPRESS and associated logos are trademarks and/or registered trademarks of Bellwether Media, Inc.

Editor: Elizabeth Neuenfeldt   Series Design: Jeffrey Kollock   Book Designer: Laura Sowers
Projects and Project Photography: Jessica Moon   Craft Instructions: Sarah Eason

Printed in the United States of America, North Mankato, MN.

TABLE OF CONTENTS

Throw a Lunar New Year Party! .. 4
Paper Lantern................... 6
Paper Orange................... 8
Stir-fry Noodles................10
Delicious Dumplings............14
Jade Juice.....................16
Egg Carton Dragon..............18
Glossary......................22
To Learn More..................23
Index.........................24

THROW A LUNAR NEW YEAR PARTY!

Lunar New Year is a festival that began in Asia. Today, it is celebrated by people around the world! The holiday lasts for 15 days in late January and February. Families gather to celebrate. They eat big meals, honor **ancestors**, and enjoy fireworks.

You can celebrate the arrival of a new year with a Lunar New Year party! The activities in this book have been designed to honor favorite **traditions**, from decorative lanterns to tasty dumplings. So let's get ready to throw a Lunar New Year party!

TOP TIP

Look for this feature throughout the book. It will give you tips to help improve your projects.

MATERIALS AND TOOLS

To make your party projects, you will need some basic art supplies, such as colored cardstock and paper. You will also need some basic kitchen tools, including knives, forks, spoons, cutting boards, and mixing and serving bowls.

You will also need:
- glue
- scissors
- pencils
- markers
- paints
- paintbrushes
- tape

PAPER LANTERN

Extra materials needed:
1 sheet of orange letter-sized paper
scissors
stapler

The Lantern Festival happens on the last day of Lunar New Year. People hang colorful lanterns from their houses and on the streets. Many write riddles on their lanterns. Those who guess the right answer may get a prize. You can make lanterns for your party with this fun craft!

1 Cut a 0.5-inch (1-centimeter) strip off of the end of your paper and put it to one side.

2 Fold the remaining paper in half.

PAPER ORANGE

Extra materials needed:
orange paper
green paper
yarn

Oranges and tangerines are common sights during Lunar New Year! Many people believe they bring luck and happiness. Their bright color also **symbolizes** wealth. The Chinese words for "orange" and "tangerine" also sound like the words for "wealth" and "luck." Bring some luck to your party with these fun decorations!

1 Take an orange piece of paper and cut it in half. Fold each piece back and forth like an accordion.

2 Staple each folded piece of paper at the center.

3 Staple the two paper pieces together at the center.

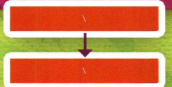

4

Pull up the left and right sides of the top paper pieces and glue together.

pull and glue

5

Glue the left side of the top paper piece to the left side of the bottom paper piece. Then glue the right side of the top paper piece to the right side of the bottom paper piece.

pull and glue

pull and glue

6

Your model should now look like this. Set aside, and then cut two leaf shapes from your green paper.

7

Glue one leaf onto the right side of your model. Then, loop a length of yarn and glue it to your leaf, as shown.

8

Glue the other leaf on top. Then fully pull out the orange paper and glue into position. Use the string to hang your paper orange!

pull and glue

FINAL

STIR-FRY NOODLES

Extra materials needed:
1-inch (2.5- centimeter) piece of fresh ginger, peeled
2 garlic cloves
4 tablespoons ketchup
3 tablespoons oyster sauce
2 tablespoons soy sauce
1 red pepper
1 green pepper
2 chicken breasts
2 tablespoons sunflower oil
1 cup bean sprouts
1 packet of fresh egg noodles
4 green onions
wok or large frying pan

Longevity noodles are a popular Lunar New Year food! Cooks may **stir-fry** them or serve them in broth. They are traditionally cooked as one long strand, which represents long life. Eaters slurp up the noodles so they do not break them. Breaking them is bad luck! Try making these tasty stir-fry noodles as a main dish for your party!

SAFETY TIP

Ask an adult to help you with this recipe!

Grate the ginger and garlic and put it in a bowl with the ketchup, oyster sauce, and soy sauce. Stir together and then put to one side.

Cut the red and green peppers into slices.

Chop the chicken breasts into small, bite-sized chunks.

Pour the oil into a wok or large pan and heat on the stove at a high temperature. Once hot, add the chicken and stir regularly. Cook until the chicken starts to brown.

TURN THE PAGE!

5
Add the peppers and cook for a few more minutes.

6
Add the sauce you created in Step 1 and stir well.

7
Add the bean sprouts and the noodles. Snip in the green onions. Cook the entire mixture for a few more minutes until everything is heated through, then serve.

TOP TIP

You can serve your noodles with chopsticks or with forks!

FINAL

DELICIOUS DUMPLINGS

Extra materials needed:
1 1/2 cups ground pork
1 teaspoon grated ginger
1 teaspoon sesame oil
1 tablespoon vegetable oil
1/4 cup soy sauce
5 green onions
6–8 Chinese cabbage leaves
pinch of salt
1 large egg
16 dumpling wrappers
1/2 cup water
frying pan with lid
extra green onions, toasted sesame seeds, and soy sauce for garnish

Making dumplings together is a family tradition for many during Lunar New Year. The dumplings are shaped like old Chinese money called ingots. Eating dumplings is said to bring wealth! Some people even hide a coin in one of the dumplings. Whoever finds it will have the most **prosperity** in the upcoming year. Try making dumplings for your friends and family!

SAFETY TIP
Ask an adult to help you with this recipe!

1. Place the ground pork, ginger, chopped green onions, sesame oil, and soy sauce in a bowl. Marinate in a fridge for a few hours.

2. Chop the cabbage leaves into small pieces and sprinkle salt on top. Set aside for 30 minutes, then squeeze out any moisture.

14

3 Add the cabbage and egg to the pork mixture and mix together.

4 Put a tablespoon of the mixture into the center of a dumpling wrapper. Wet the edges of the wrapper with water.

5 Fold the wrapper over and pinch the edges together to seal. Then pinch pleats along the edges to create a pouch.

6 Heat the vegetable oil in the large frying pan. Cook the dumplings for 2 to 3 minutes on each side. Add water and cover the pan with a lid. Cook for 5 minutes. Place the dumplings on a plate and sprinkle with sesame seeds and green onions. Serve with a soy sauce dip.

FINAL

JADE JUICE

Extra materials needed:
1 cup fresh spinach
1 cup water
handful of frozen pineapple chunks
handful of frozen mango pieces
1 banana, chopped
blender

Jade is a hard stone prized for its beautiful color, most often green. It is thought to bring luck and wealth. This makes it a popular gift for Lunar New Year. People also wear jade jewelry to keep bad luck away. This tasty drink shares jade's green **hue**. See if it will bring luck to you and your guests!

1 Add the spinach and water to your blender cup, then blend.

2 Add the pineapple, mango, and banana to the mixture.

3

Blend the mixture well. Repeat Steps 1 through 3 so that there is enough juice for all of your party guests. Serve immediately.

FINAL

TOP TIP

Serve your jade juice in a tall glass with a patterned drinking straw.

EGG CARTON DRAGON

Extra materials needed:
2 egg cartons
red and yellow paint
2 googly eyes
black marker
1 yellow pipe cleaner
2 red pom-poms
yellow cardstock
orange cardstock
yellow crêpe paper

Dragon dances are popular events during Lunar New Year! They began in China. The dragons represent China and are thought to bring luck. During the dances, teams of dancers carry a long dragon. They move it in smooth, winding motions. See if you can make a dance with the dragon from this activity!

1 Cut the first egg carton in half and paint both pieces red. Let dry.

2 Cut two sections from the bottom of the second egg carton and paint them yellow. Let dry.

3 Once dry, glue the bottom of the first egg carton to the top section at an angle, as shown.

4 Glue the yellow section on top to make the dragon's eyes.

5 Glue googly eyes onto the yellow section and use a black marker to add nostrils to the red section.

6 Take a yellow pipe cleaner and fold it in half. Glue a red pom-pom onto each end and let dry.

TURN THE PAGE! ▶

TOP TIP

If you do not have googly eyes, you can draw or paint your dragon eyes instead.

10

Glue the flames to the sides of your dragon's head. Finally, glue some of the crêpe paper strips to the mouth of your dragon to look like flames.

FINAL

GLOSSARY

ancestors—relatives who lived long ago

dragon dances—traditional Chinese dances that often happen during festivals; during a dragon dance, one or two people use poles to control the head of a large dragon puppet while other dancers move its long, snakelike body.

hue—color

longevity—related to something that lasts a long time

prosperity—success and wealth

stir-fry—to prepare food by frying it in oil while stirring often

symbolizes—stands for something else

traditions—customs, ideas, or beliefs handed down from one generation to the next

TO LEARN MORE

AT THE LIBRARY

Katz Cooper, Sharon. *Chinese New Year.* North Mankato, Minn.: Pebble, 2021.

Loh-Hagan, Virginia. *Nian, the Chinese New Year Dragon: A Beauty Tale: Adapted from a Chinese Legend.* Ann Arbor, Mich.: Sleeping Bear Press, 2020.

Wallace, Adam, and Andy Elkerton. *How to Catch a Dragon.* Naperville, Ill.: Sourcebooks Wonderland, 2019.

ON THE WEB

FACTSURFER

Factsurfer.com gives you a safe, fun way to find more information.

1. Go to www.factsurfer.com.
2. Enter "Lunar New Year party" into the search box and click 🔍.
3. Select your book cover to see a list of related content.

INDEX

Asia, 4
China, 8, 14, 18
delicious dumplings, 14–15
dragon dances, 18
dumplings, 4, 14
egg carton dragon, 18–21
February, 4
ingots, 14
jade, 16
jade juice, 16–17
January, 4
Lantern Festival, 6
longevity noodles, 10
materials and tools, 5
oranges, 8
paper lantern, 4, 6–7
paper orange, 8–9
safety tip, 10, 14
stir-fry noodles, 10–13
tangerines, 8
top tip, 5, 7, 13, 17, 19

All photos in this book are provided through the courtesy of Calcium.